THE OUTB

A selection of classic Australian poetry with contemporary Australian photography

PRINCIPAL PHOTOGRAPHY

John Meier

ADDITIONAL PHOTOGRAPHY

Lorrie Graham
Peter Jarver
Carolyn Johns
Philip Quirk
Grenville Turner

Spirit of the Land

Angus&Robertson
An imprint of HarperCollins*Publishers*

Australian Poets' Biographies

JAMES CUTHBERTSON 1851–1910

Born in Scotland, as a young man Cuthbertson held a position in the Indian Civil Service and studied at Oxford. He came to Australia at the age of 23 and spent the rest of his working life teaching Greek and Latin at Geelong Grammar School in Victoria, and writing verse.

VICTOR DALEY 1858–1905

Though working at various times in his life as a clerk, a newspaper freelancer and an unsuccessful gold prospector, Daley mostly attempted to live by his writing, and as a consequence he often suffered poverty. As well as the poetry published under his own name, he also wrote social commentary under the name of Creeve Roe.

GEORGE ESSEX EVANS 1863–1909

English by birth, George Essex Evans emigrated to the Darling Downs in Queensland as a young man to start a new life as a farmer. He later went on to be a teacher, a public servant and to work in newspapers. A prolific poet, Evans is known for his patriotism and for his great sympathy and admiration for the early pioneers in Australia.

MARY HANNAY FOOTT 1846–1918

Born in Scotland, Foott came to Australia as a young girl. Upon the death of her husband, an outback station owner, she became the literary and social editor of the *Queenslander*, a post she held for 10 years. She is best known for her ballads.

ADAM LINDSAY GORDON 1833–1870

While Gordon received some critical acclaim during his lifetime, he only gained wide acceptance following his suicide due to his inability to cover the printing costs of his last book of poetry. He had suffered melancholia for several years and though he had some success as a politician and horseman, he had also experienced publishing and business failures. A commemorative bust of Gordon was installed in Westminster Abbey, London, after his death.

EMILIE MANNING HERON ("AUSTRALIE") 1845–1890

As well as writing poetry, Heron was also a journalist and contributed to several British and Australian publications, including the *Sydney Morning Herald* and the *Illustrated Sydney News*. A strong advocate for women's access to higher education, her work was published under the name "Australie".

HENRY LAWSON 1867–1922

Though he was born in a tent on a goldfield in rural New South Wales and has a reputation as a bush poet, Henry Lawson spent most of his life in the city. Forays into the bush, and memories of his early life in the country inspired much of Lawson's writing, both poetry and short stories. One of Australia's best known writers, he was nurtured early in his career by his mother Louisa who published his poems in her own publications.

LOUISA LAWSON 1848–1920

Publishing only one book of poetry, Louisa Lawson concentrated her energies on social reform. She set up the journal *The Republican* and later *Dawn*, the first Australian magazine catering solely to women's interests. She also helped establish the Dawn Club which was active in the women's suffrage movement. She was also the mother of the well-known writer, Henry Lawson.

JOHN SHAW NEILSON 1872–1942

Lacking a formal education, and constantly dogged by poverty, John Shaw Neilson found a voice as a lyric poet while travelling Australia seeking work. The son of a poet who had fallen on hard times, Neilson spent most of his life as a labourer – shearer, farm hand, quarryman, roadmender and mine worker – yet in that time also managed to pen an impressive collection of poetry, sometimes having to dictate to fellow workers because of his failing eyesight.

A.B. "BANJO" PATERSON 1864–1941

One of Australia's most loved poets, Banjo Paterson wrote the majority of his poetry before the age of 40. He also had a successful legal career, was a war correspondent during the Boer War, went on to be a journalist in Australia and later lent his knowledge of horsemanship to the First World War effort, rising to the rank of major. He is best known for such works as *Waltzing Matilda* and *The Man from Snowy River*.

WILLIAM CHARLES WENTWORTH 1790–1872

Famous for undertaking the first crossing of the Blue Mountains in New South Wales (along with Blaxland and Lawson), Wentworth also had active and influential legal and political careers, was a prominent landowner and helped found the University of Sydney. In 1824 he co-founded the newspaper the *Australian*.

FRANK WILMOT ("FURNLEY MAURICE") 1881–1942

Born in Collingwood, Wilmot managed a book store and later took up a position at Melbourne University Press. At the turn of the century he published a monthly magazine *Microbe* using his own press. Wilmot was the winner of the Melbourne Centenary Poetry Prize and for most of his life published under the name "Furnley Maurice".

GEORGE ESSEX EVANS

from *The Sundowner*

When the track is hot and the plain is dry,
When the glare is fierce and the sun is high,
I doze and doze till the morn is o'er;
Then I straighten up and I start once more,
And up goes bluey and billy and Jack,
And my feet are padding the dusty track.

KIMBERLEY REGION, WESTERN AUSTRALIA

Parachilna, South Australia

LOUISA LAWSON

from *The Lonely Crossing*

A man on foot came down to the river,
A silent man, on the road alone,
And dropped his swag with a chill-born shiver,
And sat to rest on a wind-worn stone.

A.B. "BANJO" PATERSON

from *Black Swans*

From the northern lakes with the reeds and rushes,
    Where the hills are clothed with a purple haze,
Where the bellbirds chime and the songs of thrushes
Make music sweet in the jungle maze,
They will hold their course to the westward ever,
Till they reach the banks of the old grey river,
Where the waters wash, and the reed beds quiver
In the burning heat of the summer days.

LAKE MOURNPALL, VICTORIA

DERBY, WESTERN AUSTRALIA

HENRY LAWSON

from *The Great Grey Plain*

Out West, where the stars are brightest,
	Where the scorching north wind blows,
And the bones of the dead seem whitest,
	And the sun on a desert glows –
Out Back in the hungry distance
	That brave hearts dare in vain –
Where swagmen tramp for existence –
	There lies the Great Grey Plain.

ADAM LINDSAY GORDON

from A *Dedication*

In the Spring, when the wattle gold trembles

'Twixt shadow and shine,

When each dew-laden air draught resembles

A long draught of wine;

When the sky-line's blue burnish'd resistance

Makes deeper the dreamiest distance,

Some song in all hearts hath existence,–

Such songs have been mine.

ARKAROOLA, SOUTH AUSTRALIA

FLINDERS RANGES, SOUTH AUSTRALIA

FRANK WILMOT ("FURNLEY MAURICE")

from *The Agricultural Show*

The lumbering tractor rolls its panting round,

The windmills fan the blue; feet crush the sand

FRANK WILMOT ("FURNLEY MAURICE")

from *The Agricultural Show*

Here is a world that stands upon sun and rain
In a humid odour of wool where the sheafing grain
Falls like pay in the palm.

MT KOSCIUSKO, NEW SOUTH WALES

FLINDERS RANGES, SOUTH AUSTRALIA

A.B. "BANJO" PATERSON

from *Australian Scenery*

A land, as far as the eye can see, where the waving grasses grow
Or the plains are blackened and burnt and bare, where the false mirages go
Like shifting symbols of hope deferred – land where you never know.

A.B. "BANJO" PATERSON

from *Australian Scenery*

Land of plenty or land of want, where the grey Companions dance,

Feast or famine, or hope or fear, and in all things land of chance,

Where Nature pampers or Nature slays, in her ruthless, red, romance.

STRZELECKI TRACK, SOUTH AUSTRALIA

MT ISA, QUEENSLAND

A.B. "BANJO" PATERSON

from *Australian Scenery*

And we catch a sound of a fairy's song, as the wind goes whipping by,

Or a scent like incense drifts along from the herbage ripe and dry

– Or the dust storms dance on their ballroom floor, where the bones of the cattle lie.

MARY HANNAY FOOTT

from *Where the Pelican Builds*

They had told us of pastures wide and green,
To be sought past the sunset's glow;
Of rifts in the ranges by opal lit;
And gold 'neath the river's flow.
And thirst and hunger were banished words
When they spoke of that unknown West;
No drought they dreaded, no flood they feared,
Where the pelican builds her nest!

PINE CREEK, NORTHERN TERRITORY

STURT STONY DESERT, SOUTH AUSTRALIA

HENRY LAWSON

from *Out Back*

For time means tucker, and tramp you must, where the scrubs
and plains are wide,
With seldom a track that a man can trust, or a mountain peak to
guide;
All day long in the dust and heat – when summer is on the track –
With stinted stomachs and blistered feet, they carry their swags
Out Back.

WILLIAM CHARLES
WENTWORTH
from *Australasia*

Thence far along Nepean's pebbled way,
  To those rich pastures, where the wild herds stray, –
The crowded farm house lines the winding stream
On either side, and many a plodding team
With shining ploughshare turns the neighb'ring soil,
Which crowns with double crop the lab'rer's toil.

MT RESCUE CONSERVATION PARK, SOUTH AUSTRALIA

KANANGRA WALLS, NEW SOUTH WALES

VICTOR DALEY

from *The Martyr*

And riders were galloping gaily
        With loose-held flowing reins,
Through dim and shadowy gullies,
        Across broad, treeless plains

GEORGE ESSEX EVANS

from A *Drought Idyll*

The hay was done, the cornstalks gone, the trees were dying fast.
The sun o'erhead was a curse in red, and the wind was a furnace blast;
The waterholes were sun-baked mud, the drays stood thick as bees
Around the well, a mile away, amid the ring-barked trees.

LAKE ARGYLE, WESTERN AUSTRALIA

KOSCIUSKO NATIONAL PARK, NEW SOUTH WALES

EMILIE MANNING HERON

("AUSTRALIE")

from B*odalla*

Ah, Comerang! shall I picture thee at morn,
While still the valley sleeps in robe of mist.
And lowing cows of varied hue and form
Thro' frosty fields are driven to the sheds,
Where childish milkmaids, rosy-faced and bright,
With skilful hands press out the creamy milk?

JAMES CUTHBERTSON

from *The Bush*

Give us the wattle's gold
    And the dew-laden air,
And the loveliness bold
    Loneliest landscapes wear.

These are the haunts we love,
    Glad with enchanted hours,
Bright as the heavens above,
    Fresh as the wild bush flowers.

CAPE YORK PENINSULA, QUEENSLAND

EYRE PENINSULA, SOUTH AUSTRALIA

HENRY LAWSON

from *The Never-Never Land*

By homestead, hut, and shearing-shed,
  By railroad, coach, and track –
By lonely graves where rest our dead,
  Up Country and Out Back;
To where beneath the clustered stars
  The dreamy plains expand –
My home lies wide a thousand miles
  In the Never-Never Land.

HENRY LAWSON

from *The Never-Never Land*

It lies beyond the farming belt,
    Wide wastes of scrub and plain,
A blazing desert in the drought,
    A lake-land after rain;
To the skyline sweeps the waving grass,
    Or whirls the scorching sand –
A phantom land, a mystic realm!
    The Never-Never Land.

BARROW CREEK, NORTHERN TERRITORY

UPPER TUMUT RIVER, NEW SOUTH WALES

JOHN SHAW NEILSON

from It Has Come in the Corn

The heads of the barley can whisper but never could sing,
And the oats only rustle, as many birds out on the wing;
The wheat is in laughter, it cannot be calm in the Spring.

GEORGE ESSEX EVANS

from *At the Base Hospital*

The willows sweep the water, and the rushes lean a-down,

And I see the river shining far away,

With a snowy cloud above it, floating softly, like a crown,

And the water-hen and wildfowl at their play.

LAKE HATTAH, VICTORIA

FINKE RIVER, NORTHERN TERRITORY

A.B. "BANJO" PATERSON

from *With the Cattle*

The plains are all awave with grass,
    The skies are deepest blue;
And leisurely the cattle pass
    And feed the long day through;
But when we sight the station gate,
    We make the stockwhips crack,
A welcome sound to those who wait
    To greet the cattle back

ANONYMOUS

from *The Old Bullock Dray*

So it's roll up your blankets,
And let's make a push,
I'll take you up the country,
And show you the bush.
I'll be bound you won't get
Such a chance another day,
So come and take possession
Of my old bullock dray.

FRENCH ISLAND, VICTORIA

FLINDERS RANGES, SOUTH AUSTRALIA

VICTOR DALEY

from *His Mate*

No faintest sign of distant water glimmered
    The aching eye to bless;
The far horizon like a sword's edge shimmered,
    Keen, gleaming, pitiless.

A.B. "BANJO" PATERSON

from *White Cockatoos*

Now the autumn maize is growing,
  Now the corn-cob fills,
Where the Little River flowing
  Winds among the hills.
Over mountain peaks outlying
  Clear against the blue
Comes a scout in silence flying,
  One white cockatoo.

OATLANDS DISTRICT, TASMANIA

FLINDERS RANGES, SOUTH AUSTRALIA

JOHN SHAW NEILSON

from *The Ballad of Rembrance*

And he would talk as men will talk of what their hands have done,

Of plains and hills and the wilderness where sheep and cattle run,

Of the bitterness of frost and rain and the blinding of the sun.

A.B. "BANJO" PATERSON

from *On Kiley's Run*

The roving breezes come and go
    On Kiley's Run,
The sleepy river murmurs low,
And far away one dimly sees
Beyond the stretch of forest trees –
Beyond the foothills dusk and dun –
The ranges sleeping in the sun
    On Kiley's Run.

FLINDERS ISLAND, TASMANIA

LAKE HATTAH, VICTORIA

GEORGE ESSEX EVANS

from An *Australian*

Symphony

The grey gums by the lonely creek,

The star-crowned height,

The wind-swept plain, the dim blue peak,

The cold white light,

The solitude spread near and far

Around the camp-fire's tiny star,

The horse-bell's melody remote,

The curlew's melancholy note,

Across the night.

A.B. "BANJO" PATERSON

from *Barney Devine*

Out on the cattle camps waiting for light,
Watching the stock in the hush of the night,
Singing your songs of the bush and its ways,
Telling your tales of the wandering days.

LASCELLES DISTRICT, VICTORIA

KIMBERLEY REGION, WESTERN AUSTRALIA

A.B. "BANJO" PATERSON

from *Clancy of the Overflow*

And the bush hath friends to meet him, and their kindly voices greet him

In the murmur of the breezes and the river on its bars,

And he sees the vision splendid of the sunlit plains extended,

And at night the wondrous glory of the everlasting stars.

Principal Photography

JOHN MEIER is influenced by the painters and the composers of the romantic period. He endeavours to portray the spiritual qualities of Australia's wild places. John is a principal of Precious Planet Wilderness Photography. His photographs can be found on pages 8, 11, 15, 16, 19, 20, 27, 31, 32, 36, 39, 44, 47, 51, 52, 56, 59 and 60.

Additional Photography

LORRIE GRAHAM is a photo-journalist whose assignments often take her throughout Australia. Her photographs can be found on pages 7 and 35.

PETER JARVER is an award-winning landscape photographer best known for his images of the Northern Territory and its spectacular lightning displays. One of his photographs can be found on page 48.

CAROLYN JOHNS is based in Victoria and is best known for her film and portrait work. She is a founding member of Wildlight Photo Agency. Her photographs can be found on pages 12 and 64.

PHILIP QUIRK is a landscape photographer represented in many major public collections throughout Australia and is a founding member of Wildlight Photo Agency. His photographs can be found on pages 43, 55 and 63.

GRENVILLE TURNER photographs the Australian landscape and documents the environment and Australian wildlife. He is a founding member of Wildlight Photo Agency. His photographs can be found on pages 23, 24, 28 and 40.

Angus&Robertson
An imprint of HarperCollins*Publishers*, Australia

First published in Australia in 1995

HarperCollins*Publishers*
25 Ryde Road, Pymble, Sydney NSW 2073, Australia
31 View Road, Glenfield, Auckland 10, New Zealand
77–85 Fulham Palace Road, London W6 8JB, United Kingdom
Hazelton Lanes, 55 Avenue Road, Suite 2900, Toronto, Ontario M5R 3L2
and 1995 Markham Road, Scarborough, Ontario M1B 5M8, Canada
10 East 53rd Street, New York NY 10032, USA

National Library of Australia Cataloguing-in-Publication data:

The outback: spirit of the land: a selection of classic
Australian poetry with contemporary Australian photography.

ISBN 0 207 18921 8

1. Australian poetry. 2. Australia – Poetry.
3. Australia – Pictorial works. I. Meier, John (John Richard).

A821.083294

Front cover photograph by John Meier

Printed in Australia by Griffin Colour

9 8 7 6 5 4 3 2 1
99 98 97 96